Searchlight
BOOKS™

What
Is Digital
Citizenship?

Smart Internet Surfing

Evaluating Websites and Advertising

Mary Lindeen

Lerner Publications Company
A division of Lerner Publishing Group, Inc.
241 First Avenue North
Minneapolis, MN 55401 USA

For reading levels and more information, look up this title at www.lernerbooks.com.

Library of Congress Cataloging-in-Publication Data

Lindeen, Mary, author.
    Smart internet surfing : evaluating websites and advertising / by Mary Lindeen.
        pages cm. — (Searchlight books. What is digital citizenship?)
    Includes bibliographical references and index.
    ISBN 978-1-4677-9492-3 (library binding : alk. paper) — ISBN 978-1-4677-9689-7 (paperback : alk. paper) — ISBN 978-1-4677-9690-3 (pdf)
    1. Internet searching—Juvenile literature. 2. Web search engines—Juvenile literature. 3. Computer network resources—Evaluation—Juvenile literature.
4. Electronic information resource literacy—Juvenile literature. I. Title.
ZA4230.L56 2016
025.0425—dc23   2015018890

Manufactured in the United States of America
1 – VP – 12/31/15

Contents

Chapter 1

SEE THE SITES

You can have fun riding the wave of information found on the Internet. It helps to have some basic knowledge of how the Internet works. You also need curiosity and common sense. You need to know how to stay safe. That's how you surf the Internet the smart way.

You can use the Internet to access lots of information. How can you be a smart Internet user?

The Internet is the collection of networks that connects computers around the world. The Internet also connects satellites and smartphones. Most people connect to the Internet by using the World Wide Web. The web helps people find and share information online.

Many phones connect to the Internet.

You can connect to the web by using a browser. There are many different browsers to choose from. Internet Explorer is one. Google Chrome and Safari are some others.

Browsers display web pages on the Internet.

Did You Know?

No one knows for sure how the word *surfing* came to mean looking for information online. Some say it is because being online connects people to a constantly changing wave of information. This "wave" is like the ocean's constantly changing pattern of waters. Others say it is because people online tend to jump from site to site. They don't really have a plan for where they're going. This is similar to riding a wave on a surfboard. You don't know how long you'll stay up or exactly where the waters will take you. You just let the wave carry you and enjoy the ride!

Know the Address

Once you're connected to the web, you can go to millions of different websites. People all around the world are putting information online all the time. Businesses do it. Schools do it. Governments do it. All kinds of people and groups put information online.

Many businesses use the Internet to share information about themselves and their products.

It is important to keep all that information from getting mixed up. So each website has its own web address. A web address is kind of like your home address. Your home address is a special combination of numbers and words that tells people exactly where to find you. Similarly, a web address is a combination of words, letters, and sometimes numbers and special characters that tells people where to find that website.

A web address is similar to a home address.

Mailing addresses use abbreviations. For example, people use *ST* for Street or *LN* for Lane. People also use two-letter abbreviations for states, such as *NY* for New York or *TX* for Texas. Countries have their own abbreviations, such as *US* for the United States.

STREET SIGNS SOMETIMES
USE ABBREVIATIONS.

Internet addresses use abbreviations too. The abbreviation *www* stands for *World Wide Web*. Abbreviations such as *au* or *uk* tell what country a site is from. Sites including *au* are from Australia, while sites including *uk* are from the United Kingdom.

Still other abbreviations tell the kind of group a site belongs to. Sites that end in *.com* are commercial. This means they belong to a business or a group whose main purpose is to make money. Sites that end in *.edu* belong to a school. Sites with *.gov* in them belong to a national, state, local, or tribal government in the United States. Sites that end in *.org* often belong to a business or a group whose main purpose is to help people rather than to make money.

Websites that end in .gov belong to the government.

Know Who's Talking to You

Knowing who owns a website can help you decide if the information there is true and useful. For example, websites with a .com address are often selling something. They want you to buy their products or use their services. They might tell you things that are true. But they might not tell you everything you'd want to know. A website that sells bike tires might tell you exactly how to figure out when you need new tires for your bike. But it probably won't tell you if a different store sells tires just like the ones you see on the site for a whole lot less money.

If you have a question about bicycle tires, a website that sells bicycle supplies may not be the best source to turn to.

Ask yourself whether things you read online are facts or opinions.

Sites with an .org address might not be selling anything. But some of them may be trying to get you to believe the things they believe. You need to decide if a group that owns an .org website is one you can trust. You also have to decide if a website is telling you facts or opinions. Facts are statements that can be proven. You can trust facts. Opinions are ideas that people believe or think. You can choose to agree or disagree with an opinion.

Some information online is not true. Some of it is misleading. Think about what you read. Be a wise consumer of online information.

Chapter 2

SPOT THE SPAM

Have you ever found unwanted mail in your mailbox at home? Junk mail is mail you didn't ask for and do not want. It is usually mostly ads. Businesses print these ads. They send them to hundreds or even thousands of people. The companies hope that some of the people who get the ads will decide to buy something.

Unwanted mail is called junk mail. What is unwanted e-mail called?

You can get junk mail on your computer too. It is called spam. Companies send you e-mails that you did not ask for and do not want to get. Companies can do this as long as they follow the laws.

Some kinds of spam are allowed. Some kinds are not. It can be hard to find out who sends spam. Lots of companies that send illegal spam never get caught.

Spam can be annoying and can clog your e-mail inbox.

Is It Spam or Not?

You might ask a company to send you e-mails about new products. Those messages are not spam. You asked to get those messages. You might also get e-mails that you don't ask for but are glad to get. Imagine being happily surprised to get a funny e-mail from your pen pal in New Zealand. That message is not spam either.

> **Many e-mails are messages you want to receive.**

How can you tell if an e-mail is spam? Here are some clues:

- The e-mail comes from a person or a company you don't know.
- The e-mail says it comes from a person you know, but it does not seem as if it's something that the person would write.
- The e-mail looks as if it came from someone famous.
- The e-mail says that it comes from an expert who wants to help you solve a problem or share top-secret information with you.
- The e-mail tells you that you are or could be a lucky winner.

Always be careful with any message you think may be spam.

How to Deal with Spam

It is best to ignore spam messages. Do not open them. Just delete them. Opening spam messages tells the senders that your e-mail address is real and working. They will send you more unwanted messages. The sender might even sell your e-mail address to other companies. Those companies will send you even more spam. Sometimes a spam message contains a virus. Opening the e-mail lets the virus into your computer. The virus could damage your computer.

IT'S ALWAYS BEST TO DELETE SPAM MESSAGES BEFORE YOU OPEN THEM.

Some spam messages may ask for passwords or other personal information.

Sometimes people open spam messages by mistake. Most of the time, nothing bad will happen in this case. If you open a spam message by mistake, here are some tips to keep in mind:

- Do not reply to it.
- Do not click on anything in the message, such as an image or a link to another website.
- Do not share passwords or other personal information with the sender. The spammer could use that information to steal your identity or your money.

Chapter 3

FIND THE HIDDEN MESSAGES

The Internet reaches people of all ages all around the world. It is the perfect place for companies to advertise their products. And companies that want to sell things to kids use online advertising aimed at kids just like you.

Online advertisements may be directed at kids. Why would companies try to get your attention?

It might seem strange to advertise to kids. Adults are the ones who usually control the money in a family. But kids have a lot of power over the things their families buy. Kids beg their parents for things like new video games, toys, phones, and sneakers. Parents usually buy their kids at least some of the things they want. And kids with their own money to spend will buy some of the things they want too!

Businesses may try to get your attention off-line too.

Advertainment

Kids often go online looking for entertainment. They like to play games and watch videos. Advertisers know this. They try to make their ads look like entertainment. For example, a company might sponsor music videos. The company will pay part of the cost of making a video. That company gets to have its products shown in the video in return. Or the company will get to have its ads appear on-screen along with the video. You will see the ads whenever you watch the video.

You may see products in the videos you like to watch with your friends.

Advergames are video games that also sell something. Some games have characters that are company mascots. Sometimes products are used as playing pieces or prizes. Or a company's products might simply be shown in the background of a game. Kids who play these games will see these products often. They will remember these products and want to buy them.

STORES SELL PRODUCTS THAT THEY THINK WILL CATCH YOUR ATTENTION.

The Message in the Message

Kids also use the Internet to spend time with their friends. Some kids go to websites that have chat rooms. A chat room is an online site where people who are interested in the same things can talk to one another. Kids talk online by sharing comments on video game sites and social networking sites as well.

Advertisers know this. They put ads on these sites. They put comments on these sites that mention the products they are trying to sell. They also pay famous people to mention their products on these sites. Both kids and adults like to read comments posted online by their favorite actors, musicians, and athletes. Millions of fans listen to messages from the celebrities they admire. The fans might not realize that some of these messages are also ads.

Social media sites often feature advertising.

Did You Know?

You might be helping advertisers sell things online without even knowing it. Companies can get information about you when you connect to them online. How do they do that?

Remember, the Internet is a network of electronic links. When you are linked to a website, that website is also linked to you. You share information with advertisers when you do any of these things:

- "Like" something online
- "Share" something online with your friends
- Take a quiz or a survey online
- Play a game online
- Tell your friends about a new app or music video that you really like
- Buy something online
- Put any information about who you are and what you like or dislike online

Chapter 4

GET THE PICTURE

Smart Internet surfing means thinking about whether you can trust the words you are reading or the video you are watching. It also means thinking about whether you can trust the pictures you see.

The Internet is full of images and videos. Can you trust that their content is true?

Cameras are built into all kinds of electronic devices: phones, tablets, and computers. It is easy to take pictures and put them online. It is easy to share a photo with millions of people on the Internet. It is also easy to change the way the photo looks.

Photographers have always been able to change the photos they take to make the pictures look different. Photos used to be changed by hand. Computer software makes it easier than ever to change a photo. Sometimes you can clearly tell that a photo has been changed. Sometimes it's impossible to tell that you're looking at an altered image.

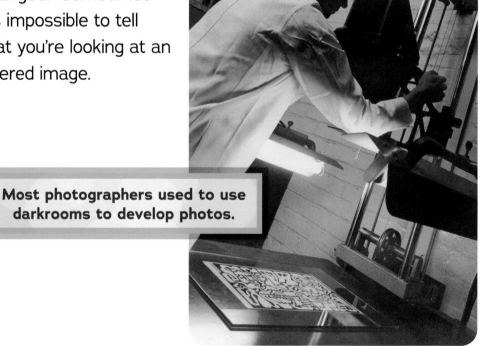

Most photographers used to use darkrooms to develop photos.

Fact or Fiction?

Someone selling something online can use photos to show you what is for sale. Sometimes the photos show things as they are. Sometimes the photos make things look better than they really are. A photo of a cracked plate can be changed to remove the crack in the picture. A photo of a rusty car can be changed to make the car look as good as new.

A photographer could edit this image to make the plate look fixed.

Photos are also used to get your attention online. Suppose a writer wants you to read an article on his website. He might include a shocking photo with the article to get your attention. The picture might be so shocking that you tell your friends about the article. They tell their friends. The writer then has hundreds of people reading his article.

But that photo might not be true. It might show something that did not really happen. It could be a mix of parts of several different photos. Or parts of the picture might have been added to or removed from the original. The picture may even have nothing to do with the article.

Many photos on the covers of magazines have been altered.

Good or Bad?

Changing a photo is not always a bad thing. Sometimes a picture has to be trimmed down to fit a certain space. Or it has to be made a little lighter or darker so the details of the photo show up better. Photos are changed for all kinds of reasons.

Most newspapers will not use photos that have been altered. They want their readers to be able to trust the news they report. Some people who post photos online feel the same way. They want you to be able to trust them and their website.

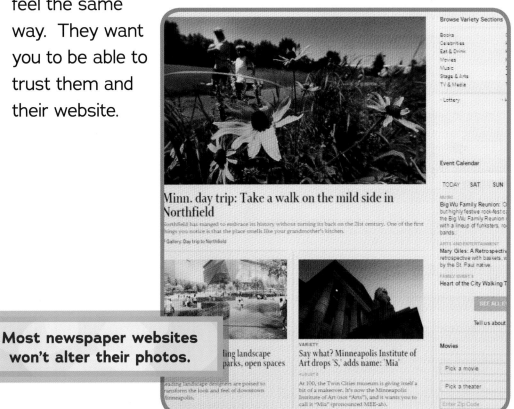

Most newspaper websites won't alter their photos.

KIDS OFTEN EDIT PHOTOS JUST FOR FUN. IT
CAN BE A WAY OF BEING CREATIVE.

But not everyone feels that way. Some people will do anything to get you to look at their website. They want photos to look a certain way to get your attention. They will change photos to make them look more interesting. Changing a photo can take a lot of creativity and skill. It can be fun.

Picture Perfect

Changing photos can also have serious consequences. For instance, fashion companies often sell their clothing by using photos of models wearing the clothes. Customers can see what the clothes look like when they are being worn. That can be helpful for customers. It can help them spend their money more wisely.

Clothing advertisements often feature models in a company's clothing.

However, fashion photos are often changed to make the models in them look different than they do in real life. A model can be made to look taller, shorter, heavier, or thinner. A photo can be changed to show a model with more muscles. The color of a model's skin, hair, or eyes can be changed. Fashion companies hope these ads will make more people want to buy their clothes. It is good for their business.

The image in this advertisement may have been altered.

But some people compare themselves to the models in the photos. They want to look like those models. They begin to feel bad about their own bodies. They develop eating disorders and other serious problems. They do not realize that photos of models often do not show what people look like in real life.

Seeing edited photos in ads can lead to a negative self-image.

Be a Good Digital Citizen

The Internet has brought many issues into our lives that people didn't have to deal with before the web came along. Yet it has also changed the world for the better. It has connected people around the globe. It has solved many problems.

You can learn to be a smart Internet surfer. Just remember to think about what you find online. Ask questions about where websites come from. Look for reliable sources. Look for facts and opinions. If you do these things, you will be well on your way to becoming a good digital citizen!

When you're careful and use common sense, using the Internet is lots of fun!

Technology and the Digital Citizen

Wouldn't it be great if the cooks in your school's lunchroom served only foods you liked? Or if stores carried only clothes that looked good on you? It would make life easier if someone filtered out things you didn't want. Then you could focus on the things you like best. When it comes to e-mail, such sorting is possible. A spam filter is software that sorts e-mail before you read it. It can stop spam from getting mixed in with e-mails you want.

There are many kinds of spam filters. They all work in a similar way. A spam blocker scans incoming e-mails. It looks for words, word patterns, and sender information common to spam. It identifies messages that have those features. Then it blocks those messages from your inbox.

The filter does not delete blocked messages. It sends them to a separate e-mail folder. You can open that folder to see what messages were blocked.

Sometimes a spam filter will accidentally send a message you want into the spam folder. But you can move the message into your inbox. Blocking software looks for patterns in those messages you move. Then the filter adjusts its controls so it makes fewer mistakes in the future.

Glossary

advertise: to give information about something you want to sell

browser: a computer program that lets you find and look through web pages and other data

fact: a piece of information that is true

image: a representation, such as a picture or a statue

link: a connection between one web page and another

mascot: a person, animal, fictional character, or symbol used to represent a group

network: a system of things that are connected to one another

online: controlled by or connected to a computer or network

opinion: the ideas and beliefs that a person has about something

social networking site: a website that allows you to interact with other people

virus: hidden instructions within a computer program designed to destroy a computer system or damage data

website: a location connected to the Internet that has one or more pages on the World Wide Web

LERNER
SOURCE

Expand learning beyond the printed book. Download free, complementary educational resources for this book from our website, www.lerneresource.com.

Learn More about Smart Internet Surfing

Books

Bodden, Valerie. *Identify and Evaluate Advertising*. Minneapolis: Lerner Publications, 2015. This book will help you learn more about identifying advertising so that you'll know online ads right away when you see them.

Cosson, M. J. *The Smart Kid's Guide to Using the Internet*. Mankato, MN: Child's World, 2014. This selection provides advice for smart and safe Internet use, including safe searching and safe use of social media.

Minton, Eric. *Spam and Scams: Using Email Safely*. New York: PowerKids, 2014. Learn about the risks that come with having an e-mail account and what steps people can take to protect themselves.

Websites

KidsHealth—Safe Cyberspace Surfing
http://kidshealth.org/kid/watch/house/internet_safety.html
This site helps readers learn how to protect their privacy and avoid dangerous strangers online.

KidSmart—Being Smart Rules!
http://www.kidsmart.org.uk/beingsmart
This website provides facts, videos, posters, quizzes, and other interactive activities to help readers navigate safely online.

PBS Kids—Webonauts Internet Academy
http://pbskids.org/webonauts
Visit this website to play a game that teaches readers how to stay safe as they explore cyberspace.

Index

Photo Acknowledgments

The images in this book are used with the permission of: © Nivek Neslo/The Image Bank/Getty Images, p. 4; © iStockphoto.com/skynesher, p. 5; © iStockphoto.com/gmutlu, p. 6; © iStockphoto.com/rhyman007, p. 7; © Cultura RM/Getty Images, p. 8; © Nico Tondini/Masterfile/CORBIS, p. 9; © Snap Decision/Photographer's Choice/Getty Images, p. 10; kids.gov, p. 11; © Pamela Moore/E+/Getty Images, p. 12; © iStockphoto.com/SilviaJansen, p. 13; © Bobbo's Pix/Alamy, p. 14; © Mike Kemp/Tetra Images/Brand X/Getty Images, p. 15; © Paul Bradbury/Caiaimage/Getty Images, p. 16; © Hero Images/Digital Vision/Getty Images, p. 17; © iStockphoto.com/EHStock, p. 18; © iStockphoto.com/scyther5, p. 19; © iStockphoto.com/pixdeluxe, p. 20; © DreamPictures/VStock/Blend Images/Getty Images, p. 21; © iStockphoto.com/PeopleImages, p. 22; © Zero Creatives/Cultura RF/Getty Images, p. 23; © iStockphoto.com/mactrunk, p. 24; © JGI/Blend Images/Getty Images, p. 26; © iStockphoto.com/Wavebreakmedia, p. 27; © Arthur Tanner/Hulton Archive/Getty Images, p. 28; © iStockphoto.com/red2000, p. 29; © iStockphoto.com/numbeos, p. 30; StarTribue.com, p. 31; © PeopleImages/E+/Getty Images, p. 32; © Robert Landau/Alamy, p. 33; © Kathy deWitt/Alamy, p. 34; © Zia Soleil/Getty Images, p. 35; © Marc Romanelli/Blend Images/Getty Images, p. 36.

Main body text set in Adrianna Regular 14/20.
Typeface provided by Chank.